CAMBRIDGE INTRODUCTION TO WORLD HISTORY
GENERAL EDITOR · TREVOR CAIRNS

Life in the Old Stone Age

SECOND EDITION

Charles Higham

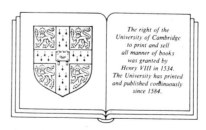

*The right of the
University of Cambridge
to print and sell
all manner of books
was granted by
Henry VIII in 1534.
The University has printed
and published continuously
since 1584.*

CAMBRIDGE UNIVERSITY PRESS
Cambridge
London   New York   New Rochelle
Melbourne   Sydney

Imaginary reconstructions by Murray Webb
Other drawings, maps and diagrams by Tom Cross,
Peter Taylor, Keith Howard and Banks and Miles

Other illustrations in this volume are reproduced by kind permission
of the following:
front cover, p.48, Axel Poignant; back cover, p.17, Australian News
and Information Bureau; pp.2, 3, 26, 28, 42, 46, 47, Time-Life, Inc.;
pp.4, 9, 11, 13, British Museum (Natural History); p.5, High
Commissioner for New Zealand; p.15, Mansell Collection; p.16,
photograph by Dr K. Birket-Smith, National Museum, Copenhagen;
p.29, reconstruction by M. M. Gerasimov, Novosti Press Agency;
p.37, Foto Mas, Barcelona; p.39, Hutchinson Publishing Group Ltd
and Alfred A. Knopf, Inc.

front cover: *An Australian Aborigine poised ready to launch his
spear from a throwing device known as a womera. Hunting
peoples have used these throwers since they were introduced
during the Magdalenian era, which began somewhere
between 15,000 and 12,000 BC and continued until about
8000 BC.*

Published by the Press Syndicate of the University of Cambridge
The Pitt Building, Trumpington Street, Cambridge CB2 1RP
32 East 57th Street, New York, NY 10022, USA
10 Stamford Road, Oakleigh, Melbourne 3166, Australia

© Cambridge University Press 1971, 1979

First published 1971
Reprinted 1972, 1975, 1976
Second edition 1979
Fourth printing 1986

Printed in Great Britain by
Ebenezer Baylis & Son Ltd, Worcester and London

ISBN 0 521 21869 1
       (0 521 07048 1 first edition)

Note to the second edition

Ideas on this topic are often revised in the light of new finds.
Minor revisions have been made throughout the text and there
are eighteen new drawings. The two major alterations in this
edition are the introduction of another type of early man in the
evolutionary sequence, to take account of the archaeologists'
present view of human development and revision of the dating
in line with recent research. The name Thinking Man no longer
refers specifically to the type of man to which we belong today
but to the newly-introduced ancestor – *Homo sapiens*.

*By 40,000 years ago Latest Man
as we know him today was living*

Contents

80,000 years ago, ...anderthal Man was living.

By 250,000 years ago, Thinking Man was living.

By 1,500,000 years ago, Upright Man was living.

By 2,500,000 years ago, Handy Man was living.

1 THE DISCOVERY OF THE OLD STONE AGE

About 150 years ago, when the cuttings and tunnels of the first European railway systems were being constructed, and when the gravel deposits laid down by ancient rivers were being dug out to provide building material for homes and roads, workmen used occasionally to find, buried deep underground, curious looking stone weapons and bones of unknown animals.

Such things were found in Britain, France and Germany. In all those countries the same questions were being asked. How old are these stone weapons? Who made them? Why are they found deep underground in gravel quarries?

At first, all sorts of answers were given. Some said that the tools must have been left by people known only to folklore, or by people mentioned in the Bible, or even that they were made by elves or fairies. Others thought that an ancient and primitive type of man, who lived by hunting the strange animals whose bones had also been found, had made them as weapons. Such men were described as belonging to a 'Stone Age', because the weapons found were always made of stone. When in 1854 a drought caused the level of lakes in Switzerland to fall, the remains of ancient wooden houses were found. These houses contained beautifully shaped and finished stone axes quite different from those found in the gravel pits. The primitive tools were therefore said to belong to the 'Old Stone Age', and the others to the 'New Stone Age'.

A further question about the primitive stone tools had to be answered. Why were they covered by deposits of gravel sometimes more than 30 metres (100 feet) thick, and how did the gravel get there? The answer to this question was simple, but most unexpected. They had been buried as a result of a series of ice ages.

This flint handaxe from Swanscombe, in southern Britain was found in the same gravel bed as the human remains known as Swanscombe Man, and, like them, is about 250,000 years old. is of the Middle Acheulian type, more refined than the basically similar tool used earlier. The handaxe was probably a general-purpose tool, and was eventually supplanted by tools shaped especially for particular jobs. Similar axes have been found on prehistoric sites in Europe, Asia and Africa. Stone tools quite similar to handaxes were used until recently by Aborigines in Australia.

The effects of an ice age

Some people today live in a warm climate, but others have to burn coal, oil or gas to keep warm during the winter. Imagine what would happen to people living in Europe if the climate began to get colder than it is today. It would snow and hail much more, and, instead of melting, snow would build up into huge drifts. In the mountainous regions, such as the Alps or the Pyrenees, these drifts would be so big that they would turn into ice under their own weight and spill over into surrounding valleys, driving rocks and stones in front of them, like giant slow-moving rivers. In time, a polar ice cap would cover the countryside. These slow-moving masses of ice – or glaciers – would cut away the soil in their path. They would carry it into the plains, where it would be swept away by swollen rivers, fed by melting ice at the glaciers' edges. The cold would kill trees, and force animals to move away in search of warmer lands. Some rivers would turn into torrents with the melting ice, and others would dry up if the water found a new way to the sea. Men's homes would be destroyed. People too would have to move to warmer lands, or adapt themselves to the cold, as the Eskimos have done in northern Canada.

Further south, the effects of the increasing cold would be less severe, but just as important for all living things. An ice age in the north would probably be accompanied by a rainy period further south, while, with the retreat of the ice, the south would become dry again.

Fortunately for us, such changes in climate would take place very slowly. Yet, during the Old Stone Age, the great glaciers in northern Europe advanced and retreated at least seven times. We can talk, therefore, of a number of separate ice advances taking place during the Old Stone Age. Of course, the ice did not cover the whole world, but only regions around the North and South Poles, or high mountain ranges. Near the Equator, there were simply rainy and dry periods.

How a glacier is formed

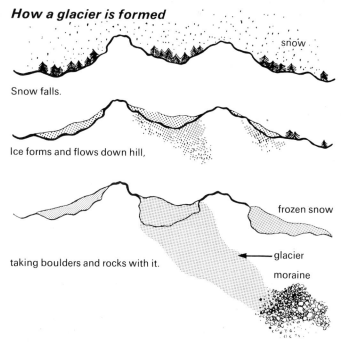

snow

Snow falls.

Ice forms and flows down hill,

frozen snow

taking boulders and rocks with it.

glacier

moraine

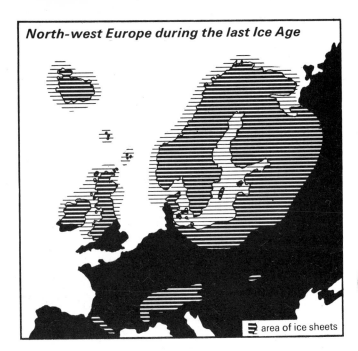

North-west Europe during the last Ice Age

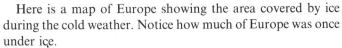
area of ice sheets

A mammoth and a woolly rhinoceros based on drawings found at Font de Gaume, France, which were made by men of the Old Stone Age about 25,000 years ago.

Here is a map of Europe showing the area covered by ice during the cold weather. Notice how much of Europe was once under ice.

The return of the warm weather

Now think of the warm weather returning. Gradually the ice would melt and the glaciers shrink, or even disappear. A vast, barren land would be left, but this would soon change as first grasses, and then trees returned. The rivers, no longer swollen by melting glacier water, would settle into regular channels, while animals would be attracted back by the plentiful herbage.

How do we know there were ice ages?

People who have studied the landscape in Britain, Europe and America, are certain that there were periods in the past when it was sufficiently cold for ice to form, and glaciers to spread. They have pointed out that ice, as it moves along, can push huge boulders in front of it. When the ice finally melts, these boulders are left in a jumbled line called the 'end-moraine', which marks the limit of the ice cap. We know this because it is possible to

study the behaviour of ice today in certain parts of the world. Rocks which could only have come originally from Norway have been found in such a moraine in southern Britain. This suggests, therefore, that ice formed in northern Norway and then spread southwards, bringing huge boulders with it. When the summer temperatures improved, the ice melted and left such stones stranded like beach pebbles after a high tide.

Another fragment of evidence for the existence of ice ages is that the bones of animals normally existing in cold climates have been found where the weather is now warm. In Britain, for example, the bones of the mammoth and woolly rhinoceros have been discovered. These animals have long since died out following the return of warm weather to which they were not accustomed.

Now that we have outlined the effects of an ice age, it is easy to see why the tools and animal bones have been found deep in gravel pits. The great rivers, fed by melting ice, laid down thick layers of gravel. The abandoned camps of ancient hunters

ould then have been covered by such rivers, and tools or bones
ft behind in the camps would have been carried along and
nally deposited among the gravel on the river bed.

After the discovery of Old Stone Age tools in the European
ravels, archaeologists began to search for similar remains in
ther parts of the world. Dr Louis Leakey, for example, worked
 Africa; and between 1935 and 1975 he and his colleagues
und many ancient camp sites such as those at Olduvai Gorge,
 Tanzania.

The geologists tell us how the Olduvai Gorge deposits were
id down. There was a lake where the Gorge was later formed.
irst, lake sediments accumulated over the lava from an ancient
olcanic eruption. Then further layers were built up by the wind
epositing fine sands and volcanic ash, or the lake forming
uds. Men of the Old Stone Age lived beside the lake and
eakey found that their camp sites were clearly visible, one on
 p of the other, in the many layers which are preserved in the
 des of the Gorge. The oldest was occupied almost two million
ars ago.

The Old Stone Age was a time of gradual change. For more
an two million years, the great ice caps developed, spread and
rank, and, like a great hand, they moulded the earth's surface
 we know it today. Animals also changed. While some died
ut altogether – you cannot see a live mammoth today – others
rived. Over one million years ago, central Africa was
opulated by animals such as giant hippopotami and giraffes
hich were much bigger than those there today. They have now
sappeared, either through dying out during unfavourable
eather conditions, or by developing gradually into modern
imals, bearing little resemblance to those of long ago.

Occasionally, fragile bones of men who lived during the Old
one Age have been discovered. From these bones we can tell
at we have developed from creatures which we might not
cognise as being even distantly related to us, were we to see
em today. What did those men look like? What sort of lives
d they lead?

Remains from the river bed

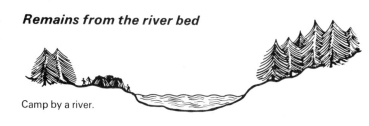

Camp by a river.

The camp is flooded by the river, swollen with meltwater
from the glacier, and tools left there are swept away.

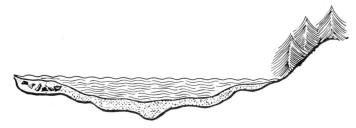

Downstream the river flows slower and the tools, with stones
and gravel, drop to the bottom.

The tools remain, covered by gravel, several miles from the
original camp; eventually the river level falls, and the tools
are left as part of the river bank.

2 THE MEN OF THE OLD STONE AGE

The bones of men who made the tools and weapons described in chapter 1 were first found by chance. Cave explorers and gravel diggers sometimes found the bones of long-extinct animals, together with what looked like human bones. These excited the interest of many people during the early part of the nineteenth century. Although the bones looked human, they were in many ways different from those of any modern man. Indeed, one learned professor declared that a skull found at Neanderthal in Germany could only have come from an idiot. Another ancient skeleton, which was discovered in the Welsh cave of Paviland, also caused much controversy. Some people thought that the skeleton belonged to an extremely distant period of time. Others, such as the respected Dean Buckland, claimed that it was buried there by Roman soldiers a mere 1,900 years ago.

Man 'created' in 4004 BC

The reason why many leading scholars refused to accept that such human remains could be so very old was because they believed that man had been created looking as he does today. They valued the opinion of Archbishop Ussher, who lived 300 years ago. He was convinced, from close study of the Bible, that the creation took place in the year 4004 BC. The early discoveries of fossil man, therefore, were all said to represent people living after that date, while the discovery of primitive stone tools and extinct animal bones in the caves once occupied by man was said to result from their being washed in by the great flood of Noah's time.

Before long, however, the discovery of human bones together with those of the woolly rhinoceros and mammoth at Spy in Belgium and La Chapelle in France led many people to ask whether Archbishop Ussher's date of 4004 BC was correct, or whether man had existed on earth for far longer than had previously been believed.

Remember that the shape of the bones we are talking about differs from that of any bones from living men. Should the creatures in question, then, be called men at all?

Before answering this difficult question, we must think carefully what distinguishes us from our closest relatives, the chimpanzee and gorilla. Not long ago, it was thought that man alone made tools to help to defend himself or to obtain food more easily. But now we know that chimpanzees also use tools. Jane Goodall, for example, has lived with chimpanzees in the Gombe Stream Reserve in Tanzania and described how they use grass stems to poke into termites' nests and fish out the insects to eat. They also make 'sponges' from chewed vine leaves, to obtain water from where it collects in hollows in tree trunks. Other scholars have suggested that man differs from his close relatives because of his ability to hunt animals for their meat, but the chimpanzee and baboon also hunt small animals.

Nowadays, most archaeologists agree that man, while closely related to the chimpanzee and gorilla through sharing a very distant common ancestor, has developed certain skills particularly well. He can use language to communicate, is very skilful at making many useful tools, and is a fast runner on two legs, which makes him able to hunt effectively. He has a much bigger brain than a chimpanzee, and can remember and plan ahead better. Males and females form long-lasting bonds, called marriage, to bring up children and teach them how to survive, and they have developed the habit of sharing their food between members of the same family, or between friends.

Now, as we go backwards in time, we find that the earlier the type of man, the smaller was his brain and the simpler were his tools. But we can recognise a time, about two and a half million years ago, when our ancestors had most, if not all, of the characteristics which today distinguish man from the apes.

Early men with large brains

During the last 120 years, European archaeologists have found many ancient skulls of men who had brains as large as our own ut who also had massive brow ridges and jaws. One of these kulls, from Swanscombe in England, and another from teinheim in Germany, are about 250,000 years old.

We now recognise an important fact. In Europe the escendants of the Swanscombe people had the same large rains but their faces became broader, and their brow ridges rew more pronounced. Indeed, these people became so robust hat we give them a special name, after the Neander Valley in ermany where their bones were first discovered.

On the right you can see a typical Neanderthal skull compared ith that of a modern man. Look at the massive, bony ridges ver his eye sockets, and the long flat skull. The bones of his rm show that he possessed a fearsome grip, and, although he ould not have stood more than 1½ metres (5 feet) high, careful xamination of Neanderthal skulls show that he had particu- rly powerful jaws and neck.

Neanderthal Man lived between about 80,000 and 40,000 ears ago. Archaeologists working recently in other parts of the orld have also found the bones of other large-brained men ho lived from 250,000 years ago to about 40,000 years ago. here are African examples from the Cape to the editerranean. Note, for example, this skull found at Broken ill in Zimbabwe (then Rhodesia) in 1921. It has a distinctive elf of bone over the eye sockets. Similar large-brained skulls ave been found in Indonesia, China, Russia and the Middle ast, but there have so far been no finds in America or ustralia. Few of these skulls, however, belong to such robust en as those found in Europe. Perhaps people in Europe eveloped such large jaw muscles and wide faces in response the cold, glacial climate.

We thus find that from about 250,000 years ago the old world as occupied by people whose brains were as large as modern an's but whose muscles were much stronger than ours.

Vhat happened to Neanderthal Man?

he answer to this question is 'we are not sure'. Some rchaeologists feel that he gradually evolved into people like urselves in Europe. Most experts, however, agree that modern

he drawings of the skulls are one-eighth of the original size. The constructions are in the Natural History Museum, London. e living men would probably have had a great deal of hair.

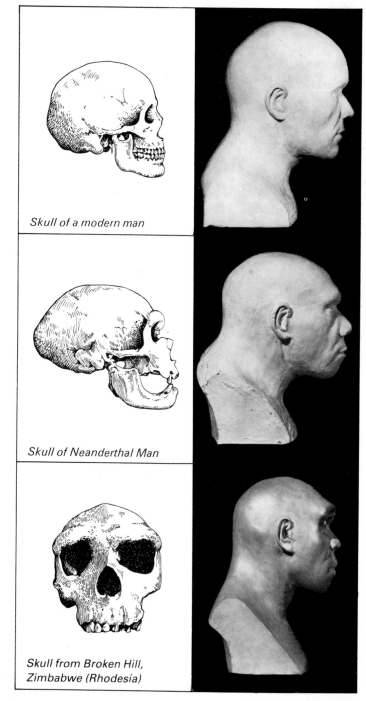

Skull of a modern man

Skull of Neanderthal Man

Skull from Broken Hill, Zimbabwe (Rhodesia)

man evolved elsewhere, perhaps in the Middle East, and then gradually colonised Europe, taking over the best hunting grounds until Neanderthal hunters themselves became extinct.

Because our ancestors had brains as large as ours by about 250,000 years ago, we call them *Homo sapiens* or Thinking Man. This does not imply that men who lived before them did not think, but rather suggests that from 250,000 years ago people were as intelligent as we are today. Neanderthal Man in Europe was just one regional type of Thinking Man.

The Missing Link: theories and discoveries

The expression 'Missing Link' was coined to describe the sort of creature which might have lived before Thinking Man. People thought he might have looked like a cross between a man and an ape: ape-like to look at, but able to make tools.

Early in this century Eugene Dubois, a Dutchman, decided that it was time people actually looked for the remains of the Missing Link, instead of simply talking about him, or drawing imaginary pictures. He chose to explore Central Java because of its wild and inhospitable nature, and the presence there of tribes of primitive hunters. Dubois's courage was rewarded with success. After much effort, he found the top of a skull and part of a thigh bone buried deep in gravel which was much older than any containing the bones of Thinking Man. He observed that the thigh bone resembled that of Thinking Man but that the top of the skull was much flatter, and the eye sockets were protected by a huge bony shelf. Moreover, the skull itself had held a smaller brain than that of any modern person.

When Dubois claimed that he had discovered the Missing Link, the stay-at-home scientists in Europe dismissed him as a madman and a forger. Poor Dubois became discouraged in the face of such criticism, refused to believe that the bones were genuine, and hid them. Thirty years passed before more discoveries in Java confirmed his theory.

Meanwhile a cave had been discovered in China containing some bones of more than twenty primitive people. These bones were like those found in Java by Dubois and were found together with extremely simple stone tools. These bones were described in great detail by a Dr Weidenreich.

It was a good thing that he worked so thoroughly, because the bones were dispatched by train to Beijing (Peking) after his study, and were lost on the way. The original bones, therefore, can no longer be seen, and experts have to work from plaster copies made from Dr Weidenreich's measurements. seems incredible that these precious bones, having lain in the ground for half a million years, were lost as soon as they were found.

'Upright Man'

Scientists now call the type of man found by Dubois *Homo erectus*. *Erectus* means that he walked upright rather than on fours. Let us, therefore, call him Upright Man. Bones belonging to this type of man have been found over much of the world the map opposite shows. A fine example of the jaw of Upright Man comes from the Mauer gravel pit, near Heidelberg Germany, and another skull was found recently in a Greek cave at Petralona. A further complete skull of Upright Man was discovered in 1975 when Richard Leakey, son of Dr Louis Leakey, led an expedition in search of human remains to the eastern shores of Lake Turkana (formerly Lake Rudolf). This skull has been dated to about one and a half million years ago.

You can see from the picture how Upright Man appeared in life. His brain was smaller than ours and he would have stood about 1½ metres (5 feet) tall. Notice the great shelf of bone over his eyes, and his powerful neck. Upright Man had little or no forehead and his mouth jutted out from his face rather like an animal's snout. Although Upright Man was similar in some respects to early Thinking Man he lived much earlier in time and made much simpler types of stone tools. The similarity between the skull and limb bones of the two types of man, however, suggested strongly that Upright Man was our ancestor.

Just as the discovery of Neanderthal Man in the nineteenth century triggered off a search for the Missing Link, so the discovery of Upright Man led people to ask if he too had human ancestors.

The earliest toolmaker of all

In South Africa, there are rich mines from which limestone has been taken for many years. The stone is blown up with

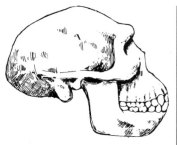

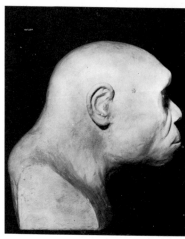

The drawing of the skull of Upright Man is one-eighth of the original size. The reconstruction of the head is in the Natural History Museum, London.

Places where Upright Man's remains have been found

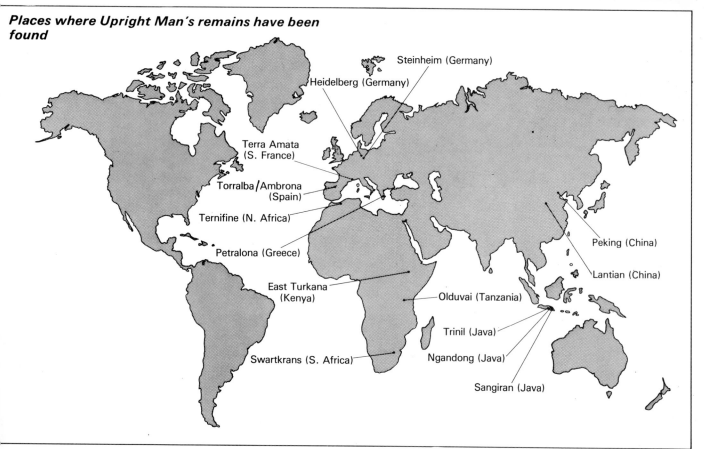

Steinheim (Germany)

Heidelberg (Germany)

Terra Amata (S. France)

Torralba/Ambrona (Spain)

Ternifine (N. Africa)

Petralona (Greece)

East Turkana (Kenya)

Olduvai (Tanzania)

Peking (China)

Lantian (China)

Trinil (Java)

Ngandong (Java)

Swartkrans (S. Africa)

Sangiran (Java)

explosive charges, and then mechanical grabs fill lorries with the crumbled rock. After the blasting, it is not unusual to find bones embedded in the stone, and an interested geologist once noticed that some were shaped like modern baboon skulls. People began to collect the baboon remains, and one collector came across a piece of fossilised skull which had an unusual shape; it was being used as a paperweight by one of the mine foremen! When the skull was measured, it showed that the brain size of the dead creature had been larger than that of even a modern baboon. The skull belonged, in fact, to a creature halfway between an ape and a primitive human.

Interest aroused in the 'Southern Ape'

In 1925, Professor Raymond Dart, the first to notice this skull, called the creature in question the 'Southern Ape'. Although he, like Dubois, was ridiculed when he suggested that it might belong to a primitive human being, he encouraged his friends to search for other examples. Soon some teeth were found by a schoolboy, in a cave at Sterkfontein, and in 1938 the bones of thirty-five individuals were discovered at a place called Kromdraai Farm.

At first, it was not clear whether this creature was ape or human. Detailed studies of the bones and stones found within the same layers of limestone as the bones of the Southern Ape suggested that he hunted the baboon, but did not make stone tools. Instead, he may have used the bones of dead animals lying around him to break open baboon skulls, so that he could eat the delicious brain inside.

A surprising discovery in East Africa, however, next suggested strongly that the Southern Ape did manufacture tools of stone. In 1959, Dr and Mrs Leakey were excavating at the bottom of Olduvai Gorge. Imagine the excitement of the two diggers when they discovered fragments of skull similar to those found by Professor Dart in South Africa. They called the skull 'Nutcracker Man', because of its huge teeth. The excitement must have been even greater, however, when stones were found which had been deliberately sharpened, in the same level as the skull. Could it have been that Nutcracker Man was, in fact, the earliest of all humans?

This question did not take long to answer for, two years later, the Leakeys found the skull of yet another primitive ape-like creature. Close examination of the newly discovered bones by

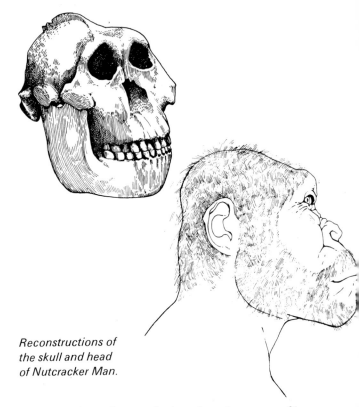

Reconstructions of the skull and head of Nutcracker Man.

experts led to the conclusion that they came from a mor intelligent being than the Southern Ape (the family to whicl Nutcracker Man is now thought to belong) but one which live at the same time and made the tools. They have called thi creature *Homo habilis* or 'Handy Man', because he was able t chip fragments of stone into a sharp cutting tool.

After the Leakeys reported the Olduvai skull, their so Richard decided to look for similar finds on the eastern edge o Lake Turkana. He found the remains of a human skull whicl was similar to Handy Man from Olduvai. Meanwhile, Leakey colleague, Glyn Isaac, excavated the bones of a hippopotamu which he found together with some chipped stone tools. Othe archaeologists have looked for very early human bones in th Omo Valley and the Afar depression in Ethiopia. They too hav been rewarded with many important discoveries, including th remains of six people who died together for reasons we canno at present explain.

What did Handy Man look like? New finds show us tha

Handy Man had a larger brain than the Southern Apes, but his jaw bone was smaller. Close study of the available limb bones also shows that Handy Man's hands and feet enabled him to walk upright and carefully manipulate small objects.

How did Handy Man develop?

Some of the research workers in Ethiopia and Kenya have tried to reconstruct the sort of environment in which these early men lived, by studying the animal bones and plant remains found in the same layers. These finds have shown that the Southern Ape and early men were evolving at a time when forests were thinning into grasslands due to a new drier climate. By about 2·8 to 2·5 million years ago, some man-like creatures seem to have started scavenging for meat or killing small animals, while their close relatives, the Southern Apes, continued as vegetarians.

By two and a half million years ago some of these very early people learnt that they could cut up the bodies of dead animals with the aid of stone chipped to a sharp edge. This discovery gave them a great advantage, because they could now quickly cut through tough skins and remove meat before scavenging lions and hyaenas arrived.

The chances of survival greatly increased for Handy Man as he developed a good memory and, through language, could warn of danger or discuss how best to obtain food. Memory and language both require a bigger and more efficient brain. So, very gradually, our ancestors changed. Their brains expanded, they grew taller, and became better tool makers. Being successful at defending themselves, their numbers increased. They spread into new lands and discovered how to adapt to a changing animal and plant world around them.

The changing story of man's evolution

In the last ten years research has revealed much important new evidence which has increased our understanding of modern man's evolution. As research continues and more exciting discoveries are made, we will need to go on modifying our ideas in the light of any more new evidence. However, at the moment, most archaeologists think that man's evolution probably followed this path:

This basalt pebble tool was found by Dr Leakey in the lowest level of Olduvai Gorge, Tanzania, in 1959. Originally believed to have been made by Nutcracker Man, we now think it was made by Handy Man, about 1·75 million years ago.

after HANDY MAN and his contemporaries (about 2·5 million years ago)
came UPRIGHT MAN (about 1·5 million years ago)
then THINKING MAN (about 250,000 years ago)
who was the ancestor of both
    NEANDERTHAL MAN (about 80,000 years ago)
and, later,
    OURSELVES (about 40,000 years ago)

Men of each type, while more intelligent and able than their predecessors, also show that they developed from them. Thus, we can assume that there must have been halfway forms – creatures combining some features of the earlier type and some of the later type. It also follows that one type of man did not suddenly die out once the next type was in existence. For example, although the earliest evidence we now have of Upright Man is about 1·5 million years ago, there is also evidence of Handy Man still living around 1 million years ago. For a period of roughly 500,000 years bands of Upright Men were probably living in parts of Africa still inhabited by bands of Handy Men.

Let us now examine the exciting story of our development from our ancient ancestors by looking at four of these types of men.

3 LIFE AS A HUNTER

You may find it surprising that it is possible to find out anything at all about life in the Old Stone Age. The great length of time involved, the changes in the appearance of the earth brought about by the action of glaciers and volcanic eruptions, as well as the effects of wind and rain, make it seem impossible for us to know what it was like to live so long ago. Try to imagine the length of time we are talking about. Most of you will know your grandfathers well, and some your great-grandfathers. Your great-great-grandfather may have lived in the middle of the nineteenth century, and you would have to say 'great' thirty-three times to get back to your ancestor who lived 900 years ago. But to return to the end of the Old Stone Age, you must say 'great' 480 times, and to return to the beginning itself, the figure rises to 100,000 times. Men of one type or another have been living on earth for about 2,500,000 years. Of that time, 2,488,000 years belong to the Old Stone Age.

How do we know that it was so long ago?

One of our most difficult problems is finding out how long ago certain events took place. We may find pleasure in looking at the cave paintings left behind by the Old Stone Age hunters, but how long ago were they painted? Indeed, when were the caves lived in? Not long ago, the answer to such questions was the result of guesswork. But now we can obtain an accurate age by means of two remarkable discoveries.

The first was that a fixed amount of the carbon in any living thing – human, animal or plant – is radioactive. The level of this carbon is kept constant during life, but when the creature dies, no more radioactive carbon is taken in and that which was there decays at a known and constant rate which we can measure. From this, it is possible to calculate, with reasonable accuracy, the date of death of a particular tree or animal, as far back as

about 50,000 years. This technique of dating is known as the radiocarbon method.

The second discovery is perhaps even more remarkable. Certain scientists have found out that it is possible to obtain the age, not only of objects once living, but also of certain types of rocks. This method, known as the 'potassium–argon' technique, can be used to estimate the true age of the first men, because some of the special types of rock and the bones of Handy Man have been found together. The technique can be used to date rocks that are millions of years old, including, therefore, those from the very beginning of the Old Stone Age.

How can we tell what the countryside was like?

The types of trees and plants which surrounded the caves or open camp sites occupied by men of the Old Stone Age must have been most important to them. Even today, people living in hilly regions lead a quite different life from farmers on the plains. But how can we find out what trees and plants were living anywhere so many thousands of years ago? In the first place, we can tell a lot from the type of animals which the men of that time hunted. If, for example, we discover the bones of reindeer and musk ox in an ancient settlement, we can be sure that there were no trees at that time, because of the cold. If, on the other hand, the bones left behind include those of the elephant, we know that the climate was warm, and that trees were able to flourish. But which trees, we cannot always tell for certain.

About sixty years ago, a Swedish scientist, with the aid of a microscope, was studying soil from an ancient village. To his astonishment, he saw a number of tiny, but regularly-shaped objects mixed in with the soil itself. Being a botanist, he recognised these objects as grains of pollen. Pollen is a hard and ough, yet extremely small, part of a plant. During the summer, pollen grains are blown from trees and plants, and some are carried to other trees, which are then fertilised. Without pollen, trees could not reproduce. So much pollen is produced by the trees, however, that most of it is wasted. It falls to the earth, or into lakes and ponds. Some is even blown into caves. Not all pollen is preserved, for the soil in which it comes to rest can destroy the tiny grains; but some kinds of soil can preserve them over hundreds of thousands of years, making it possible for us to tell what trees and plants surrounded the dwellings of the men of the Old Stone Age.

What is it like to live by hunting?

The animal bones left behind at the caves and other places occupied during the Old Stone Age tell us that all meat was obtained by hunting or scavenging. No one had yet tamed the cattle, sheep and pigs which we rely on for our food today. Imagine what it must be like to live as a hunter. Do you know of any people who still live by hunting wild animals? Two hundred years ago, there were many such people, but since then their numbers have dwindled fast, and now there are hardly any real hunters left. There are, however, still the Eskimos, who live off the meat of the caribou deer, seals and whales, in the frozen north. Some of the Bushmen of the Kalahari Desert in Africa still hunt antelopes and giraffes, while the Yukaghir in Siberia live off reindeer. The kangaroo and other marsupials supplied most of the meat eaten by the Australian Aborigines when Captain Cook encountered them two hundred years ago.

Right: *North American Indians, dressed in wolf skins, stalk a herd of bison; a nineteenth-century sketch.*

Hunters of the North American Plains

Some hunters are now extinct, surviving only in legend and recorded history. When white settlers began spreading westward along the Santa Fé and Oregon trails in the nineteenth century, they had to deal with a proud, warlike people who lived by hunting bison. These hunters, known to us as American Indians, were divided into a number of distinct tribes, such as the Cheyenne and Kiowa, Comanche and Arapaho. At one time, they had hunted the bison on foot, but the Spaniards brought horses with them to America during the sixteenth century, and it was not long before the Indians obtained horses and hunted on horseback. We know a great deal about the way of life of American Indians, for much of their hunting equipment has been kept in special museums, while their hunting methods were witnessed and recorded by frontiersmen. From this knowledge, we can tell how some hunting peoples lived, and how others may have lived during the Old Stone Age.

The summer hunt

The most important part of the year for the Indians of the Plains was the summer meeting of the tribe for the co-operative bison hunt. Having spent the winter in small family groups, they travelled from near and far to take part in the festivities and the excitement of the great hunt, when prestige and fame would attend the brave. Tepees were pitched in two or three concentric circles around a central area, where the fire burned and dances were performed.

Before the arrival of white traders with guns to sell, the first steps in the hunt were to find a steep slope or even a cliff-edge and construct an avenue of stones and bushes leading up to its very rim. A herd of bison would then be watched until it was feeding at the end of the avenue. A signal would then be given, firebrands lit, and the herd stampeded down the avenue of stones and over the precipice to its death.

The bison provided nearly all the Indians' daily needs. Meat was not only eaten fresh, but also partly cooked and pounded together with fat and berries to form slabs of so-called 'pemmican'. Sealed in leather bags, the dried meat would last long enough to provide food when the hunt was unsuccessful. Bison skins were also used for the waterproof covering of tepees, for shoes, clothes and quivers. The tough sinews of the bison were used to string bows, and to sew hides together with the aid of bone needles. Even the horns were used, not only as ceremonial headdresses but also in making such simple objects as spoons and ladles.

Indians, of course, no longer hunt the bison. Indeed, the herds were almost exterminated to feed white railway-builders, and the old hunting grounds were in time turned over to cattle grazing or to corn fields.

An Eskimo hunter today. Besides his modern equipment, he still wears his traditional warm clothes and home-made wooden goggles to keep out the glare of the snow.

Eskimos, skilful hunters in the frozen wastes

The Eskimos, who live from Greenland across Canada to Alaska, are closely related to American Indians in language and looks. Of all people, the Eskimos are best able to endure the bitter cold of the Arctic north. While many have been in contact with Europeans for so long that no traces of their original way of life survive, others, who live in more remote regions, continue to live by hunting. Caribou deer, whales and seals are all killed and eaten, different weapons being made to hunt each kind of animal. The caribou, for example, migrate northward in the spring to feed on the plants which flourish during the brie Arctic summer. When autumn comes the same animals retur to the relative warmth of southerly forests. Eskimos ar accustomed to these movements of large herds of deer, and lie i wait with their stone-tipped arrows at carefully selected place such as river crossings, where the animals are sure to be caugh at a disadvantage.

The whales are hunted from boats known as umiaks, with th aid of heavy harpoons. During the depths of winter, holes a

n Australian Aborigine prepares to hurl his spear.
(See also the caption on page 2.)

ut in the ice, over which the hunters wait patiently for the nance of harpooning a seal as it comes up for air. The meat of ead animals is usually shared out equally among the families f all those taking part in the hunt, so there is no need for nyone to go hungry.

The Eskimos make clothes of skin and fur, sewn together ith animal sinew and needles made of bone. In order to keep as arm as possible during the winter, two layers of loose fitting othes are worn, each carefully tailored to suit the individual. kin boots, gloves and hoods are also worn, as well as wooden oggles to reduce the sun's glare off the snow. Eskimos live in ribou-hide tents during the summer, but larger homes of rth and wood, as well as of snow, are built for the winter.

he Australian Aborigines adapt to desert vastes

ntil recently, Australian Aborigines were hunters like the skimos, but they had a different way of life. They had no rmanent homes, but erected windbreaks or shelters of anches and leaves for the night. Nor did they need clothes owing to the warm climate. Yet their knowledge of the animals and plants around them was very great. Their lifestyle had remained unchanged for hundreds of years. They developed a unique style of art, made exciting music and had an intimate understanding of their surroundings.

The skill with which Aborigine hunters made necessary articles out of the natural substances around them is remarkable. When described by European explorers, they had no knowledge of the bow and arrow. Instead they hunted small game with expertly fashioned wooden boomerangs and heavy wooden clubs. Kangaroos were hunted with wooden spears tipped with leaf-shaped stone points. Aborigines have also been known to tip their spears with points made of broken glass bottles obtained from the Europeans. Much of their time was spent collecting wild plants and insects, which they carried in baskets of twine, fur and vegetable fibres. Aborigines were therefore constantly on the move from place to place in order to collect particular fruits as they ripened, or to waylay animals as they came to rivers or water holes to drink. It was very rare for Aborigines to lack food. Indeed, many hunter–gatherer peoples had no word for hunger in their language.

What could archaeology tell us about modern hunters?

Imagine that American Indians, Eskimos and Australian Aborigines had died out long ago, before people began writing about them, or collecting examples of their weapons and clothes. What would we know about their way of life?

In the first place, we would have to look for the remains of their homes. In the case of the Indians, one might find a number of stone arrowheads and spearheads scattered on the surface of the ground, or thrown up by the plough as it turned the soil in some part of the endless cornfields which were once Indian country. Special expeditions have been sent out to discover ancient and abandoned settlements of the Eskimos, and have been fortunate enough to find traces of houses and stone tools left behind. It would not be so easy to discover the old settlements of Aborigines, of course, because they make very simple shelters, and never stay long at the same site. Yet they have been known to occupy caves for short periods, and we would look in cave shelters for the tools they left behind.

It would, therefore, be possible to find out where the people in question lived, and, by means of radiocarbon dating, how long ago they were there. If we were fortunate enough to find pollen grains, it would be possible to discover which plants grew when the village or cave was lived in. But what could we find out about the way in which American Indians, Eskimos and Aborigines lived?

How decay spoils the picture

In the first place, nearly all the clothes, tents, wooden spearshafts and boomerangs would have decayed long ago. We would, therefore, have to rely on the materials which survive over long periods of time. Stone, as you know, is almost indestructible, and bone can also survive for many years, provided the soil in which it lies is of the right type.

We could, therefore, tell that the Indians used the bow, arrow and spear, and lived by hunting bison. We would also find the bones of horses at the villages they once lived in, and we might also believe that Indians hunted horses as well as bison. This, of course, would not be true, because horses were ridden, not hunted. The bone needles would tell us that they sewed clothing, which might or might not have been made from bison skins. Moreover, by digging very slowly and carefully into the ground where Indian arrows and bison bones were found, it might be possible to find where posts of tepees had been driven into the sub-soil.

The survival of stone tools and broken animal bones, besides paintings and carvings, would tell us much of how the Eskimos and Aborigines lived, yet there are certain things we would have to guess. We could never be sure what the men in question looked like, because only their bones would remain, and their clothes and feather headdresses, shoes and warpaint would have long since decayed. We could only guess what their religious beliefs might have been by studying their drawings or carvings.

How far can modern hunters help us to understand Stone Age hunters?

You can see that little detailed evidence of the way man lived during the Old Stone Age can have survived for very long. We have no written records of what life was like, because writing had not been invented. But from studies of the Eskimos, Indians and Australian Aborigines, we can be sure that the people who lived towards the end of the Old Stone Age would have been brave and skilful hunters, who were expert at making many articles of which no traces have survived. They would have known the seasonal movements of the animals around them, and would have used not only the flesh, but all parts of the dead animals for their essential needs. The seasons of autumn and winter, spring and summer may well have been marked by a series of feasts accompanied by dances and mime to celebrate success in the hunt, or to please the spirit world.

What about Upright Man?

It is even more difficult to know about Upright Man's way of life, because there are no people of this type living today. Thus the further back in time we go, the less we know of man's daily activities. Keeping all this in mind, we can now look at what does remain from the Old Stone Age, and what information we can gather of the way our ancient ancestors lived.

4 ON SAFARI WITH HANDY MAN

PLACE: AFRICA
TIME: TWO MILLION YEARS AGO

Handy Man

You will remember that Handy Man was the earliest of the types of man we mentioned and that he and his relatives, the Southern Apes, lived in East Africa from about two and a half million down to about one million years ago. During that immense period of time his numbers gradually increased but he remained in Africa, never straying to regions with a cold climate. Glaciers were unknown to him. To enter the cold northern lands would have spelt death to Handy Man, for he went unclothed, and had not learnt the secret of how to make fire.

Because Handy Man lived so long ago, and since so few of his remains have been discovered, little is known of his daily activities. We must rely on the evidence found at Olduvai Gorge and East Turkana, two of the rare places to have yielded the bones of Handy Man, and his tools. From these, and from what we know of the plants and animals around him, we can imagine what it was like 'on safari' with a group of these small, ape-like people.

Hunters at the lakeside

They camp beside a lake, because they collect food from its shallows, and need drinking water. The climate is warm, but, because of the cool night breezes, they have constructed a shelter of branches secured at the base with stones. They know all the reliable sources of food around them. The women use sharpened sticks to dig for roots, and collect wild harvests of fruits and nuts. They also collect frogs, fledgeling birds and water plants from the edges of the lake. The men and older children help, but from time to time the men arrange a hunting expedition which may take them from the camp for several days. They recently attacked a small troop of baboons, and the

bones of the young, old and weak baboons now litter the camp floor. They have cracked open many of the limb bones and sucked out the tasty marrow. If they encounter the large, vegetarian Southern Apes, they show no mercy. The Ape's dull wits and slow movements make him an easy prey.

The pigs come to feed

On this occasion, some of the hunters have wandered a short distance from the home camp, seeking game. See, one of them has spotted a herd of pigs about half a kilometre ($\frac{1}{3}$ mile) away. He motions silently to the rest of the group, whose members

circle round to cut off the unwary animals. Now you can se how quickly they run, each hunter occasionally stoppin behind a bush or rocky outcrop to take cover, but keeping clos to his companions for protection.

Catching a pig

At the last moment, they fan out to confine the pigs, which hav now stopped feeding and, scenting danger, trot off with the tails in the air, snorting with fright. Four of the hunter however, have cleverly detached one of the younger anima from the herd, and they scream and throw stones at the excite

work is not yet finished. The limbs of the animal are ripped apart, so that the carcase can be taken back to the camp. Once there, the bones will be split open for the marrow.

Dusk approaches, and the small group of hunters must return to their camp for the night, well away from what remains of the dead pig. Hyaenas are already gathering, and hunters have been known to be caught while near their kill, and have had to defend themselves against savage attacks from animals stronger than themselves. The experienced leader knows when best to take cover, and he leads the party away into the gathering gloom.

east as it veers headlong from its pursuers towards a gully. fter running along the edge for 100 metres (110 yards), it seeks fuge in the gully itself.

All the hunters are now on the scene, armed with their arpened spears, with which they hit the animal as it tries to amber out of the steep-sided gully. As it falls back, one man rusts his spear in the animal's mouth, and wounds it. Another rls a rock at its eye, and draws blood. The animal is rapidly eakening, and it is only a matter of time before it panics, and ears itself out. Then it is easy to finish off.

utting up the kill

he hunters at once pick up some stones which lie on the ound about them, and chip them to form a sharp cutting-ge. They then cut open the dead pig, drinking the blood and aring at the raw meat with relish. Before long, the women and ildren from the camp approach to take their share of the ast. It is hot, and the pig is now just a bloody carcase, but the

Kill or be killed

One thing you will have noticed about the way the hunters managed to kill the wild animal was that, by having a plan, they forced the animal to do a foolish thing and get trapped in the gully. Thus, although individual men were much weaker than wild boars, they could outwit the animals by thinking and planning ahead, and by acting together with their companions as a team. It was because Handy Man knew that the pig would have a tough hide that he prepared sharp flint tools to cut up the dead body. If he had tried to use his own teeth or fingers, he would never have succeeded in the time available before big and dangerous beasts, such as lions, were on the scene.

The ability to manufacture stone tools for cutting tough skins enabled Handy Man to live off the meat of wild animals instead of having a diet restricted to plants and wild berries. Such organised hunting, linked with collecting vegetable food, was the beginning of the path which led humans to control other animals as they do today. For Handy Man, life was a matter of killing, or being killed.

Important problems solved

Handy Man was indeed different from Apes, because he had worked out the answers to some important questions. He made a range of tools from stone, and probably from wood, although these have not survived. Such tools helped to kill animals and dig up roots. He brought back food to base camp to share with the old and the women and children. During the passage of time, Handy Men probably began to talk to each other, that is, they invented language. So then they could discuss future plans, for example, or teach children to make tools, or arrange to return to base camp in two days time after a hunting trip.

Their ability to talk and to remember gave them a better chance of surviving in a hostile world. The cleverer people prospered, but the dull died out. Thus gradually Handy Man developed a larger brain and a better memory. Because he was successful at hunting as well as collecting food, he could move out into new environments. So Handy Man increased in numbers. His descendants developed and began to colonise new lands until at last they spread from Africa northwards to Asia and Europe.

Two handaxes made by Upright Man. The tool on the right is later in date and much better made. Both drawings are about two-thirds of the actual size.

PLACE: SPAIN
TIME: 500,000 YEARS AGO

High in the mountains of Central Spain, a settlement once occupied by Upright Man has been discovered. Herds of elephant used to migrate up to that height during the summer, to escape the heat of the lowland valleys. But they were tracked down by bands of determined hunters, hunters who looked very different from modern human beings. Burnt dark by the sun, long-haired and naked, they encamped by the valley of Ambrona, and hunted large and dangerous beasts with their pointed spears.

Similar bands of hunters occupied much of Africa, extensive tracts of Asia, and migrated along the lakesides and rivers of Europe. During much of the time that Upright Man lived, the climate was warm. He lived together with elephant and rhinoceros, deer, wild boar and horse. Woodland covered some of the hills and river valleys, and hunters occupied caves or lakesides close to the feeding grounds of the animals they killed.

Upright Man develops better types of tools

In the picture opposite, you can see two drawings of tools made by Upright Man. Remember that groups of Upright Man lived for hundreds of thousands of years, and that the shape of the tools made from one generation to the next gradually changed. Take, for example, these tools known as handaxes. The earliest form was heavy and clumsy, and the cutting-edges were irregular and jagged. With increased skill, however, handaxes were made thinner and sharper, and a number of different styles evolved.

Upright Man

23

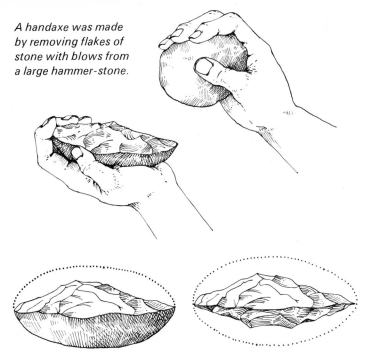

A handaxe was made by removing flakes of stone with blows from a large hammer-stone.

Could you make a handaxe?

With its sharp edges and point, the handaxe would have been an efficient tool both for cutting through the tough hide of an elephant, and for hacking meat off the carcase. How did Upright Man make such handaxes? If you live in chalky country where flint is to be found, pick up a piece, and try for yourself. You will find it much more difficult than you think. Having chosen a conveniently sized lump – or nodule – of flint, you must seek a smaller rounded 'hammer stone' with which to strike small fragments of flint off the nodule. Do this until you have outlined the shape of the handaxe on one side of the nodule, and then turn it over and begin again on the other side. Upright Man would have made a handaxe in a few minutes. See how long you take, but be careful not to cut your hands on the razor-sharp flint.

During the course of time, Upright Man found that by using a hammer of hardwood, bone or antler, instead of stone, he could chip off thin flat flakes from the nodule and therefore shape his handaxe with greater accuracy. This important discovery led to finer and more useful tools.

Upright Man's weapons

We also know that Upright Man made spears of yew wood, and had learnt to make and control fire. Having shaved the yew branch to the necessary shape, he hardened the point in the embers of his fire. A spear which might have been made by Upright Man has been found at Clacton in eastern England, while at Lehringen in Germany another spear over 2 metres (2 yards) long has been found embedded between the ribs of an elephant. We will never know for sure whether these spears were made by Upright Man, but it seems likely that they were, and certainly they fit in with our idea of Upright Man as a bold and skilful hunter.

We know he was also clever, for he used a hunting weapon known as the bolas. Special rounded stones were selected, and bound together with strips of animal hide. The stones would then have been hurled at a running animal, and have entwined themselves round its legs, bringing it to its knees. Thus, although Upright Man was not as fleet of foot as deer or swine, he used his skill and foresight to catch such animals on the run.

Some groups of Upright Man, though exactly the same in appearance as those people who made handaxes, preferred to make smaller tools for cutting and piercing animal hides. Such tools have been found in Choukoutien in China. None, however, has been discovered in Africa, where the handaxe makers ruled supreme. You can see that the two groups of

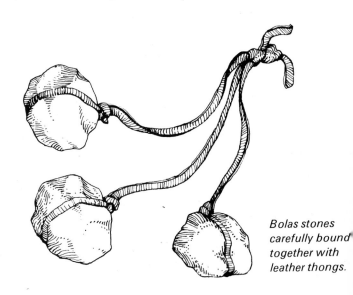

Bolas stones carefully bound together with leather thongs.

Upright Man lived over extremely wide territories, and naturally the animals they hunted and the methods they adopted in hunting varied from one region to another.

Pollen and cherrypips

We have seen how a group of hunters climbed high into the hills in Spain after the elephant. Let us now turn east, and see how Upright Man lived in China.

Pollen and cherrypips help us to understand the kind of countryside Upright Man lived in. The people who found the bones of Upright Man in China also found, in the same place, some pollen which showed that he lived among pine woods. By good fortune, some cherrypips have also been found in the caves occupied by Upright Man, which show not only that the cherry tree grew in addition to the pine, but also that Upright Man gathered cherries and brought them back to the cave for food. The woodland was also the home of wild and dangerous animals, such as the leopard and the hyaena, while the bones of rhinoceros and wild sheep, wild boar and buffalo have all been found in the caves once occupied by Upright Man.

Life at a camp site

In 1968, during the excavation of foundations for a block of flats at Nice in the south of France, Professor de Lumley found the extremely well preserved remains of huts once lived in by Upright Man. They were made of branches, sunk into the sand on the edge of a sea inlet, and each one had a hearth for cooking and to provide warmth. By carefully plotting the position of each flake of stone, de Lumley was able to tell where people had sat to make their handaxes. He even found a human footprint in the sand.

Animal bones littered the floor. Red deer, elephant and rhinoceros were hunted, and their meat brought back to be hacked off the bone and eaten. Small fragments of fishbone suggest that Upright Man was able to go into the shallows and spear fish.

A careful study of the pollen grains from this site, which is known as Terra Amata, prove that Upright Man lived there for a few weeks during the summer, then moved elsewhere. But for several years he returned for a summer stay. We know this, because he re-built his huts in the same position as the previous year, but over a thin layer of sand which had covered his abandoned home during the winter months.

If you are ever near Nice, then you can visit the Museum at Terra Amata, and see for yourself the huge animal bones and tools left there at least 250,000 years ago by Upright Man.

Who was the cleverer, Upright Man or Handy Man?

By this time groups of humans were the most dangerous creatures to be met with, because of their ability to make tools, to think and plan ahead, and to act as a team for a purpose. You might think that Handy Man and Upright Man were really very similar. Both lived by hunting and collecting, and both made simple stone tools. We suppose that Upright Man was descended from the most intelligent and capable groups of Handy Men, so that at one time the earliest Upright Man and latest Handy Man would have looked very similar. If, however, you compared the most advanced and clever Upright Man with any of his ancestors, you would at once notice a number of important differences. He had a larger and much better developed brain, and was considerably bigger and stronger. His handaxes were better made, and more efficient than the simple chipped pebbles which served the needs of Handy Man. He had learnt to control fire, and make elaborate hunting tools, such as the bolas. Upright Man was therefore more able to adapt his way of life to suit his surroundings, and we have seen how different groups of hunters were just as successful hunting deer in China as hunting elephant in Spain. This ability, together with his bravery and co-operation in hunting, ensured that men continued to increase in numbers, in strength and in intelligence.

By about 250,000 years ago the many small, slow changes had led to one big, vitally important change. People's brains were much larger – indeed, the human brain has not grown any more since then. Man with a brain of this size has been classified as a new type, *Homo sapiens* or Thinking Man, and all the people alive in the world today are of this type.

It is easy to see, then, why we cannot take one group of Thinking Men and describe their way of life as if it were typical of all. There has been far too much variety in ways of life among groups of Thinking Men – perhaps because their larger brains enabled them to think of new methods of doing things. Some sorts of Thinking Men were different from others in appearance, too; their bodies and faces were differently proportioned. So we must look at some different sorts of Thinking Men in order to try to discover how different ideas and skills were developed in different parts of this great human family.

Partly because their physical characteristics make them so easy to recognise, and partly because their remains have told us so much about the way they lived, we shall begin with the Neanderthal people.

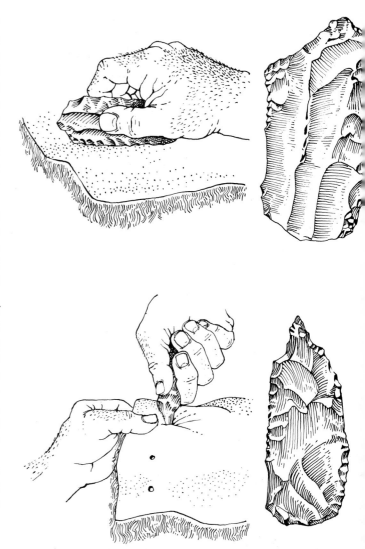

Neanderthal stone tools for scraping (above) and piercing (below) animal skins.

26

6 NEANDERTHAL MAN BRAVES THE ICE AGE

Like Upright Men before them, early Thinking Men lived over very wide territories, and the Neanderthal people were no exception. Their remains have been found across Europe from Britain to Russia, and groups seem to have spread into the northern Iranian highlands and thence westwards to the Mediterranean coast. They flourished from about 80,000 to about 40,000 years ago, and during that time there were some drastic changes in the conditions of life in many of those lands. His tools and bones of the animals he ate help us to piece together Neanderthal Man's story. Early Neanderthal Man in Europe lived during a period when the summers were warm and winters cool, then slowly the climate became worse, with winters so cold that the ice sheets began to advance over much of northern Europe. Instead of moving to the warmer lands in the south, however, Neanderthal Man adapted himself to the cold conditions, braving the ice and hunting the woolly rhinoceros and mammoth, animals well able to tolerate the cold winds which moaned continually.

But how was Neanderthal Man able to survive the depths of an Arctic winter? The answer to this question lies partly in the physical characteristics he developed to enable him to endure the cold and partly in the stone tools he made. You will remember that Upright Man made his handaxes by removing flakes from large nodules of flint, until the finished tool was formed. This process meant that many small and sharp flakes of flint were left on the ground, wasted and unwanted. Neanderthal Man, however, made use of such small fragments. With skill and care, he was able to strike from the nodule flakes of the shape he required for making various other types of tool.

This important development meant that Neanderthal Man was able to make new types of tools, and thus perform more special jobs with them than his predecessors were able to do with their clumsy handaxes. On the opposite page you can see a tool, which was carefully trimmed to form a scraper. Although we cannot definitely prove what it was used for, it seems most likely that it was made specially to scrape the fat from the inside

Neanderthal Man

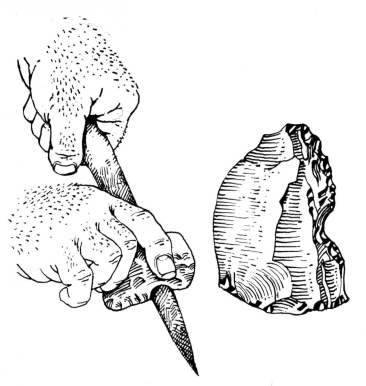

A stone tool for shaping a wooden spear point.

but, together with the knives which were also made, they would have been far more effective for seeking out and cutting the tendons and sinews which held together the bones of the hunted animals. Some of these stone points may even have been mounted as spearheads.

Without these tools, Neanderthal Man would have found it impossible to live in the cold and desolate Europe of so long ago.

The first evidence of religious feeling

One of the most interesting and important facts about Neanderthal Man is that he sometimes buried his dead companions with care and ritual. You may find this surprising in view of his brutish looks, but at a French cave called La Ferrassie, four bodies – two of adults and two of children – were found buried. Such was the reverence for the dead that the head of one of the Neanderthal bodies was carefully covered with a stone slab.

Burial of the dead becomes an accepted practice

Similar burials are quite often found in the caves once occupied by Neanderthal hunters. At es Skhul in modern Israel, for example, as many as ten bodies (each body in its own carefully-made grave) have been found in what may be the world's oldest cemetery. One of the dead men was even buried holding a joint of meat, perhaps to feed him during his life in the next world. The burial of a Neanderthal child in the Russian cave of Teshik Tash is a further example of the care and ritual often observed by Neanderthalers. After the dead Neanderthal boy had been buried there, his body was ringed by a number of goat skulls, each with the horns sticking into the ground. Many Neanderthal burials have been found in the cave of Shanidar in Iran, and the analysis of pollen from the site showed that the mourners had gathered yarrow, cornflowers and hyacinths to place beside the corpse. Who knows the reason for such ritual? This question cannot be answered with any certainty but it can be said that Neanderthal Man had come to believe that death is a beginning as well as an end.

surface of animal skins. Before the skin of an animal can be worn, the fatty tissue on the inside must be scraped off, and the skin itself thoroughly dried. The invention of such scrapers would have enabled men to dress in warm animal skins, and thus withstand the winter cold. The second type of tool shown was probably used to make holes in the skins before they were joined together to make clothes.

Neanderthal Man also made a particular form of stone scraper, specially for shaping tools from wood. The picture shows how the tool in question resembles a modern spoke shave. With the aid of this tool, spears would have been made straighter, sharper and thus more effective than was possible with the primitive tool-kit available to Upright Man. Better spears meant more success in hunting, and therefore more food for all.

Small points of stone were also made, to enable the tough hides of mammoth and rhinoceros to be pierced. These tools were smaller and more delicate than even the smallest handaxe,

28

A Russian anthropologist's model of an 8-year-old boy from Teshik Tash.

A life of danger and a violent death

Two further discoveries show, however, that Neanderthal Man still lived in a world both dangerous and cruel. One of the skeletons found at es Skhūl comes from a man who died from spear wounds. Indeed, one spear thrust had been so powerful that the top of his thigh bone was broken in two. Such a blow could only have come from a fellow man. Could the injury have occurred in a battle between rival hunting groups?

A sinister discovery from the cave of Krapina in Yugoslavia also emphasises the dangers of living at that time. The floor of the cave was found to be littered with the bones of Neanderthal Men. They had not been buried with the care seen at es Skhūl or Teshik Tash. In fact many bones had been burnt and split open. Here is strong evidence that Neanderthal Man was at times a cannibal. Perhaps in this case a rival group of hunters had been attacked and their bodies eaten.

Care of the wounded and crippled

Certain other important features of Neanderthal Man's way of life can be discovered from the dead bodies he so carefully buried. At Shanidar, the skeleton of a crippled man has been found. This may not seem important, but it shows that this man lived all his life with a withered and useless right arm, while he may well have been a burden on a society in which all food had to be collected or hunted. Yet that man lived to at least forty years of age, and would have been helped in difficult times. Unlike his ancestors, Neanderthal Man not only cared for the dead, but also for the less fortunate of the living.

Setting up a winter camp

Let us join a group of Neanderthalers towards the end of autumn, when they are preparing to set up winter quarters. During the previous months of warmer weather, one of the groups of younger hunters travelled further from the home camp than was usual, in pursuit of a wounded mammoth. As a result of the chase, they entered unfamiliar country, and after the animal had finally been tracked down and killed the hunters rested in a nearby cave front. When dawn came, the group saw that this cave was in many ways better than the one they had come from. The front of the cave was protected by a large overhanging shelf of rock, which ensured that the floor was dry, while the inside was wide and deep enough to keep out the piercing winter winds. They looked out of the cave over the

bleak rolling countryside, and noticed, with satisfaction, tha the sun would sink to the right, which meant that it would shin into the cave during the greater part of the day. One of th hunters, perhaps the boldest of them all, decided to explore th cave interior, for if the whole group of Neanderthalers including the women and children, were to move to this cave, was first of all essential to find out whether or not it sheltere bears or lions.

The cave narrowed and the roof came lower as this hunte penetrated into the hillside. Soon he was on all-fours as h scrambled over the sharp rocks and stones on the floor. On h crawled, until the flickering light from his wooden torc revealed that the passage was opening into a yawning caver with stalactites throwing eerie shadows into the gloom. By nov he was convinced that the cave was uninhabited, and turnin round he was glad to see the pinprick of light at the end of th tunnel grow larger as he approached the entrance where h companions were waiting. He told them of the cave interio and how there were no signs of the cave bear – no scratch mark on the walls made by the fearsome claws which could kill wit one blow, no hollows containing the few hairs which wou indicate that bears had hibernated there the previous winte

A new home

The decision to move camp is not taken lightly, for a number important matters have to be settled. What, for example, w the hunting prospects be like? Are there already groups hunters in the neighbourhood, and is there plentiful water f drinking, as well as for attracting wild animals?

After much deliberation, the decision is taken, and the thirt five members of the group, including tiny children and old me and women, leave the old home for the new. The weak and t old walk in the middle, protected by the strong and able me Three scouts go on ahead, seeking out possible danger. T party walks by day and sleeps at night around a blazing fire. F

Fire and footprints

After nine days' march, the new home is sighted in the distance, and the following day they reach it. The cave is all they had hoped for: it is empty, safe and dry. One man collects two sticks and twirls one between his hands into the other, until it smoulders and the tinder bursts into flame. Before long, a fire brightens the cave front.

But winter is setting in: days are getting shorter and the ground outside the cave is hard with frost. The wind howls and shrieks at night, tugging at the skin shelter that has been erected across the cave front. It is a hard time for the hunters, who go out in the raw cold, looking in the crisp snow for the footprints of any animal which, weakened by lack of food, will become their victim. In this hard climate, the weak must die to feed the strong.

ood, the hunters attack any unwary animal disturbed by their progress and gather wild plants. Yesterday the whirring bolas crippled a young deer, but no one knows if they will be as lucky tomorrow. They carry no heavy weights. A spear is enough for the men, and the women sling their babies over their shoulders, keeping them secure with leather supports.

Death in midwinter

When winter is at its deepest, an old man, now feeble but once a proud and vigorous hunter, dies. Before the corpse stiffens, his nearest relatives bind up his legs into a crouching position with leather thongs, and scoop a shallow grave in the stony soil which covers the cave floor. Women wail and chant over the body as it is laid to rest, clad in a skin cloak and accompanied by a joint of meat for its last journey. People scream and shout with sorrow, and deliberately cut themselves until the blood flows freely. After much anguish a protective stone slab is placed over the dead man's head, and the grave is filled in.

The burial is only a brief but bitter interlude in the life of the hunting camp. The waking hours are spent making tools out of flint, which is found near the cave. One man bends over a sapling, breaking off the branches, and shaves one end to a sharp point. The women are constantly active, tending the fire, or breaking open animal bones so that their children can eat the marrow. Everyone in the cave is looking forward to the spring, when the snow will melt and the days become longer. Then there will be plentiful game, and fresh berries and roots to

collect. Fish will be speared in the river and shallow edges of the lake, and the cave itself will take on a new appearance. The rough skin shelter will be taken down from the cave mouth, and newly scraped skins will be pegged out in the sun to dry. The return of the young men from hunting trips will be celebrated with feasting and dancing. But first the winter must be overcome.

Neanderthal Man was an inventor. He discovered that he could make a wide range of tools with flat flakes of flints specially chipped from the large nodules. He discovered that, by wearing the skins of dead animals, he could live in the cold as well as the warmer regions of the world. He also respected the old and handicapped. We do not know how or why this intelligent and successful variety of Thinking Man came into existence, and we do not know for sure how or why it became extinct. But the Neanderthal people seem to have disappeared as other varieties of Thinking Man appeared.

THE EMERGENCE OF LATEST MAN

es Skhūl, site of a new development

Latest Man

About 40,000 years ago, a group of hunters occupied a cave called es Skhūl, on Mt Carmel. You will remember from the previous chapter that some of the dead hunters were buried here, and their bones have been found. The skulls have slightly more pronounced brow ridges and stronger jaws than our own, but otherwise they are practically identical to us. Similar finds from the coast of North Africa suggest that around the eastern and southern shores of the Mediterranean, people very like ourselves had evolved by 40,000 years ago. This development was not, however, restricted to the Mediterranean area. In southeast Asia and East and South Africa we find a similar pattern. These modern-looking people eventually replaced all other Thinking Men and became the only type of man in the world. Scientists have called him *Homo sapiens sapiens*, meaning that he has the qualities of Thinking Man to a specially high degree. To call him Thinking Thinking Man would sound awkward, so let us call our sort of human being Latest Man.

Horse and reindeer, natural targets for a skilful hunter

To go back to the Europe of 40,000 years ago is to return to a period of intense cold. Great fingers of ice reached down from the polar north as far as the Midlands of England and the North German Plain. Wide belts of ice reached further south still, carving out wide valleys where modern rivers run. Endless plains of frozen ground, on which only lichens and mosses grew, ringed the edge of the ice, while further south were open grasslands, and then stands of pine and birch, trees able to withstand the cold. A brief summer would flicker over this land, bringing north herds of reindeer and horse, mammoth and bison, to graze the plentiful herbage. Hunting animals such as hyaenas and lions would follow to feed off the young and the weak. And finally would come the most dangerous hunters of all, bands of Latest Men. Alert, hunting in teams and occupying caves from which reindeer and horse could be silently watched and swiftly killed, they found that this was the perfect hunting ground.

By 10,000 BC the climate became much warmer. The ice sheets contracted to the north, or back to the mountain ranges where they began. You can still see the ice in the Alps, and over much of Greenland. Northwards with the ice went the cold-loving animals, such as the reindeer, which are still found living in the desolate wastes of northern Norway. Trees spread across land once deep under ice, and into the same area came new types of animals – red and roe deer, badger and squirrel. With the end of the last Ice Age, we also come to the end of the Old Stone Age itself. During the last 20,000 years of the Old Stone Age Latest Man occupied Europe, much of the Old World and, eventually, some of the New World. In that time, he invented many new types of tools and weapons, trying always to improve on those which went before. But some animals, such as the mammoth and woolly rhinoceros, either dwindled in number or died out altogether, so the hunting weapons made to kill them became redundant. During this latter part of the Old Stone Age, when Latest Man was continually developing more complex and effective tools, we can distinguish four different groups of hunters in western Europe. Each group can be identified by different types of tools and weapons. Latest Man also painted pictures of the animals he hunted, and even hunting scenes, on the walls of the caves he inhabited. Each of the four groups is also distinguishable by improvements in painting ability, and by developing art styles.

The four groups of European hunters have French names, as they were first identified in France. First came the Aurignacian group, followed by the Gravettian, the Solutrean and, finally, the Magdalenian.

The men of the first, or Aurignacian, group of hunters were responsible for the principal developments which distinguish the handicrafts of Latest Man from those of Neanderthal Man. Whereas Neanderthal Man made tools from flakes specially chipped from the parent nodules of flint, Latest Man developed a particularly skilful method of making articles from stone.

Razor blades of stone

First he would take the original nodule, and trim it carefully until its shape was long and square. Then, with the aid of wooden punch, he would strike off long, parallel-sided sections of flint, which looked rather like long razor blades. With such blades, Latest Man made a wide variety of small and highly effective tools. It was possible, for example, to make a strong but light point of stone, and mount it on the end of a spear to give it a sharper end. Small knives could also be made by mounting such blades, specially trimmed, into grooves cut into bone handles. A third type of tool, known as a burin, was manufactured to cut such grooves in bone and wood. Aurignacians also made a wide variety of stone scrapers to use in preparing skin clothing.

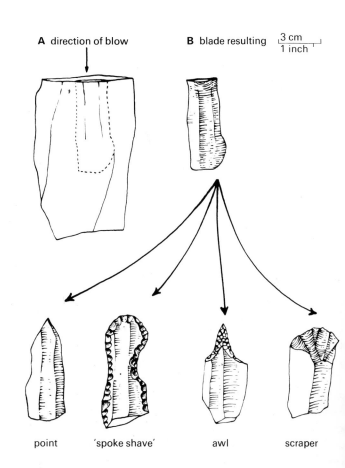

A direction of blow   B blade resulting   3 cm / 1 inch

point   'spoke shave'   awl   scraper

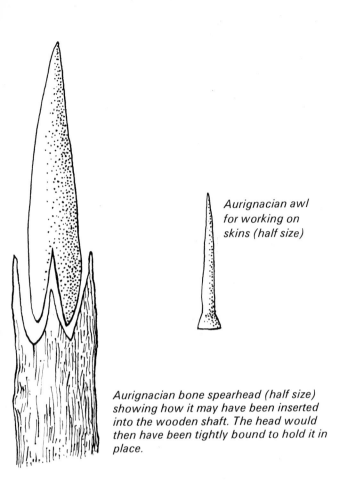

Aurignacian awl for working on skins (half size)

Aurignacian bone spearhead (half size) showing how it may have been inserted into the wooden shaft. The head would then have been tightly bound to hold it in place.

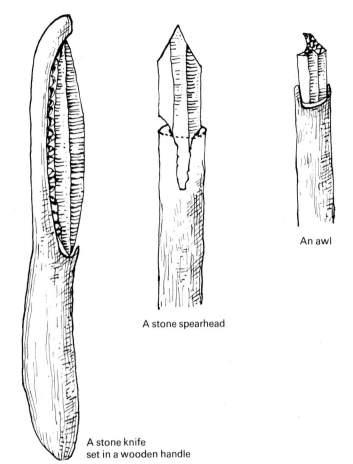

A stone spearhead

An awl

A stone knife set in a wooden handle

ools of bone as well as stone

lthough Neanderthal Man's caves were littered with the bones f dead animals, the bones themselves were rarely used for aking useful tools. Latest Man turned to bone as an bundant and useful raw material. With the aid of their knives nd burins, Aurignacian hunters specialised in the manufacture f bone points, some with a special hollow at the base to permit asy attachment to a wooden spear. They also made small bone oints or awls, with which to make the tiny holes in skins before ctually sewing them together into clothes. What a difference om the clumsy cape which satisfied Neanderthal Man.

Gravettians

The Gravettian people inhabited much of Europe, from Russia to northern Spain. Like their Aurignacian predecessors, they were skilled stone-workers, but their weapons and tools show many special features. Their knife-blades, for example, were particularly finely made, some being less than $2\frac{1}{2}$ centimetres (1 inch) long. A number of such blades would have been set into wooden handles. The Gravettians also made stone scrapers, awls and many burins, and were skilled bone-workers. Carefully finished awls made from bone or ivory make us appreciate their patience and skill.

Solutreans make long flint arrowheads and spearheads

By 17,000 BC, the Solutreans occupied much of France and northern Spain. Like the Gravettians, they too carved needles and awls from bone. They also developed particular forms of weapon. Take, for example, the characteristic stone arrowheads, or the large spearheads. Animals were now hunted with arrows as well as spears, and the Solutreans took much care in producing weapons for the chase.

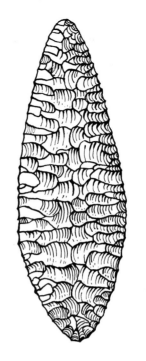

Solutrean spearhead, shouldered point, and arrowhead (half size).

Magdalenians make spear-throwers and harpoons

The Magdalenians were also descended from the Gravettian people, and although they were as skilled at stone-work as were their predecessors, they are especially notable for their skill at making articles from bone, ivory and antler. Their antler harpoon-heads, some pierced at the base for the attachment of thongs, are particularly well known. Such harpoon-heads, attached to wooden shafts, would have been used in hunting the reindeer, and the long leather thongs were to prevent a wounded but still active animal from escaping. Another advance in the field of hunting was the development of the spear-thrower, which meant that spears could be thrown further and faster. Such spear-throwers were often decorated with carved animals, like the one below which includes the representation of a mammoth.

The tools and weapons made by Latest Man in Europe show a marked improvement over those made by his predecessors. They would have helped him to lead a more successful life as a hunter, while he would also have been better clothed and equipped than Neanderthalers.

Magdalenian barbed harpoon heads of bone (half size).

A Magdalenian spear-thrower decorated with a carving of a mammoth (third size).

The discovery of cave paintings

Towards the end of the nineteenth century, a Spanish nobleman called Sautuola, who was interested in archaeology, spent much of his spare time investigating the Stone Age remains found at a cave called Altamira, in northern Spain. He took his little daughter with him on many of his expeditions to the cave, and on one occasion, while he was busily digging, he failed to notice that she had disappeared. Suddenly he heard her cries and, to his surprise, he saw her emerging from a cleft in the rock so narrow that he had hardly noticed it previously. Breathlessly, she described how she had seen pictures of bulls at the end of the cleft, where it opened out into a large cavern. At first, he found it difficult to believe her story, but she was so insistent that he decided to look for himself. He crawled along the narrow tunnel, and could hardly believe his own eyes as he saw that the walls were indeed covered with superb paintings of bison, an animal not seen in Spain for centuries.

When Sautuola reported his discovery, he was ridiculed. Who but a madman, claimed the archaeologists of the day, could believe that the savages of the Old Stone Age could possibly have executed such brilliant paintings? Sautuola must have hired an artist!

A painting of a bison from Altamira.

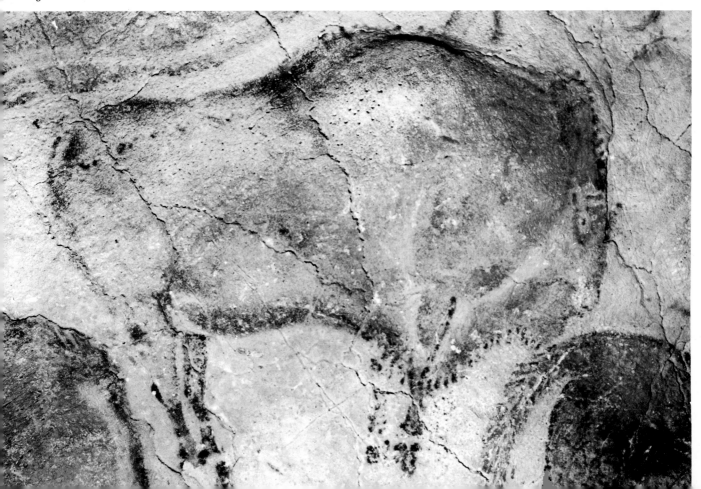

More cave paintings were found

While the experts could reject one example of cave art as being a fake, a few, who believed that Sautuola's discovery was true, set out to find more such paintings. As might be expected, more examples of cave art were soon discovered, this time at the French caves of La Mouthe and Pair-non-Pair. These convinced even the die-hard sceptics that the paintings were indeed genuine, and very old indeed.

How do we know which cave paintings were earlier than others, and which of the four groups of Latest Man was responsible for particular paintings? The answers to these two questions are surprisingly simple, if rather unexpected. In the first place fragments of rock, containing parts of a painting, have occasionally fallen off the cave wall, and become covered by the layers of broken bones and tools on the floor. We can, therefore, tell that a particular animal was painted at some time *before* those tools and bones were thrown away. Secondly, outlines of the animals painted have been found scratched on scraps of bone, executed in the same style as some of the actual paintings. Therefore, if a number of such engravings are found together with – let us say – Gravettian-type flint tools on the cave floor, and the walls of the same cave are decorated with paintings in the same style, we can conclude that the Gravettians were responsible for the art in question. Sometimes different artists painted animals, or scratched outlines of animals, over earlier paintings. By studying such superimposed paintings, we can tell which came first, and thus trace the growth and development of the art itself.

From such studies, we know that the Aurignacian people were responsible for the simplest of all paintings, which take the form of outlines of animal heads. The Gravettians showed more artistic skill, both as painters and as carvers, but the Magdalenians are recognised as the best of all, and their paintings include some finished in many colours.

Most paintings show animals

Let us see how Latest Man produced his engravings and paintings. The engravings were made with the point of a burin, while the paint was made from crushed and powdered minerals mixed with a binding liquid such as egg yolk, and applied to the cave wall with fingers, brushes of animal hair, or perhaps even

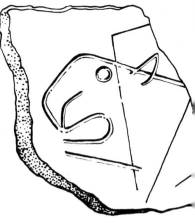

An early example of Latest Man's art. The engraved head is from an Aurignacian level at La Ferrassie, France. It is about 23 centimetres (9 inches) square.

sprayed with the aid of a pierced bone. Nearly all the finishe work represents the animals which Latest Man relied on f his food. For example, the reindeer and the horse are bo found in abundance. Wild cattle and bison are also common found, and instantly recognisable. The paintings themselv were executed with great skill and care.

Occasionally artists painted birds or fish. Perhaps the mo exciting of all paintings, however, are those of man himself. O well-known example shows a man dressed as a bison, wearir bison's hooves, tail and mask. Another famous scene, from t French cave of Lascaux, shows a hunting incident. Here th bison is shown to be horribly wounded, with his entrai hanging from his belly, but he has still managed to kill one the hunters, who, dressed in a bird-headed mask, lies dead.

Small models and carvings have been found

The art of Latest Man was not confined to the walls and ceilin of the caves which were his home. He also carved little mode of animals, and moulded animal forms from clay. On t right, for example, is a drawing of a rhinoceros's hea delicately modelled in clay. If you look carefully at t 'commander's baton', you will see the outlines of horses. Agai the most interesting models of all are those of human being These are nearly all of pregnant women, with little attentic given to the feet, hands or head. The carvers appear to ha been most concerned with the fact that the women we regnant, a fact which might be due to the hunters' wish to see the community constantly replenished with the young huntsmen upon whom so much depended.

What was the purpose of the paintings?

Why did Latest Man pay such attention to painting and engraving the animals he hunted? In discussing this question, we must remember that many paintings are found deep in the heart of the caves some distance away from where Latest Man actually lived, and sometimes in the most inaccessible of places. At Niaux, some paintings are over 1 kilometre ($\frac{3}{4}$ mile) into the mountainside. Of course, it might have been that Latest Man simply enjoyed painting in his leisure moments. But some of the animals seem to be painted with arrows sticking into them. Could it have been that these were included, striking home, in the hope that the hunt itself would prove successful? This theory is supported by a remarkable discovery from the cave of Montespan. A bear, modelled out of clay, has been found on the floor of the cave. The model has been savaged by numerous spear thrusts, which suggests strongly that the decorated caverns were used as sanctuaries, where chants, dances and mimes took place to initiate young men into the brotherhood of hunters.

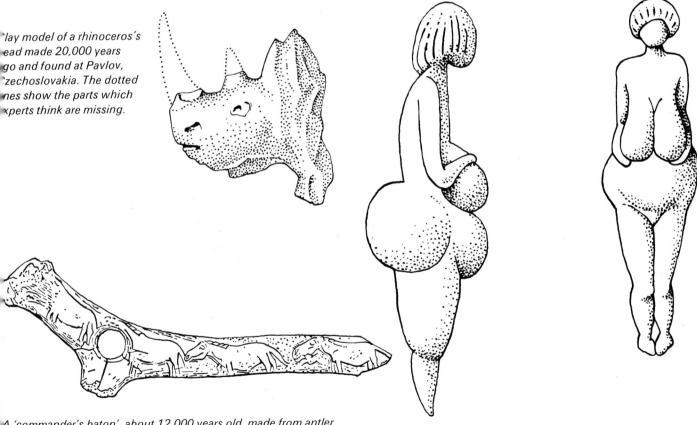

Clay model of a rhinoceros's head made 20,000 years ago and found at Pavlov, Czechoslovakia. The dotted lines show the parts which experts think are missing.

A 'commander's baton', about 12,000 years old, made from antler and decorated with engraved horses. Its use is uncertain, but it may have been used as an arrow-straightener. It was found at La Madeleine, France (quarter size).

Two carved female figurines from Lespugue, France (left) and Kostienki, Russia (right). Both are about 20,000 years old (three-quarters size).

Round the camp fire with Gravettian hunters

If it were possible to return to the Europe of 25,000 years ago, you would be struck by the open nature of the landscape. Notice how few trees there are, while grasses, lichens and mosses abound. Occasionally, you see the smoke from some hunters' camp fire, curling lazily up into the blue sky. In the evening, lions come out to hunt, followed by hyaenas and wolves, to prey on the young and weak animals. Up comes the full autumn moon, spreading unexpected shadows over the ground.

As we approach the camp fire, we can make out a cluster of tents ringing the warmth. They are made from skins, which are anchored to the ground with heavy stones and the bones of mammoth and rhinoceros. A lonely sentinel stands guard, silhouetted against the starry night sky. His spear lies beside him, and he passes the hours carving a model mammoth out of the ivory taken from an animal he himself killed.

The camp site is carefully chosen. It is sheltered from the keen north wind, but still commands a wide and open plain. During the daylight hours, herds of mammoth are visible over considerable distances. Activity begins at dawn: everyone is warmly dressed in a skin suit, carefully stitched and finished, together with a hood and fur boots, for the autumn cold is making itself felt, and a searching wind blows off the ice sheets, which may actually be seen in the distance after ten days' march to the north.

All summer has been spent hunting: it has been a successful season, but now the herds are migrating to the southern woods. Mammoth too are becoming scarcer, but enough should remain to see the winter through. Indeed, it has been decided that it is time for a party to go out and renew the traps. Although the Gravettians are skilled and brave with the spear, they catch much of their game by laying traps.

Setting the mammoth trap

The well-armed party leaves for an area in which a sizeable her of mammoth has been seen grazing over the past few days. couple of hours' march and they have arrived. The grass he has been flattened, and the soil bears the imprints of massi mammoth pads. All day is spent digging into the soft soil, f the season is not far enough advanced for it to be frozen ye When the pit is considered big enough, the top is covered ov with thin saplings and grasses and, finally, soil is laid over th completed frame. The sun is now deep in the western sky: it time to return to camp.

A meal is ready to welcome the returning band, and the me discuss the prospects for success, or go once more over the ta of how one bull mammoth was once caught in a pit trap, b managed to pull itself out in its blind rage, killing two hunters the process.

The trap is sprung, and a kill is made

Two days pass, and the trap remains untouched, but on th third day two hunters signal success: a young mammoth h tumbled into the pit, and thrashes about at the botton screaming with angry surprise at being detached from the her The hunters run nimbly to the pit, brushing aside the fir flurries of snow which bite into their faces and sting their eye They feel no sympathy for the frightened creature, now eyein them warily from below, only the need for the kill, and t pleasure in knowing that they will have plentiful meat over th next few days. They collect a heap of large stones, and begin pound the mammoth's head, aiming in particular at its eye Some men are poised ready with their spears and, with a giv signal, hurl them at the defenceless beast. Razor-sharp points flint drive deep into its head and neck, and one severs an arter

Twenty minutes suffice. Then the hunters stand back in reli gazing at the dead beast. They feel a strange emptiness arou

em now that such size and strength is no more. But there
mains much to do. They start carving off joints of meat to
ke back to the camp site. The work is hot and messy, but soon
e specially prepared skin sheets are laden with meat, slung on
ooden supports, and shouldered by the huntsmen for
ansport home. They carry away as much meat as possible, for
on wolves and hyaenas will be out, snarling and snapping
er what remains.

lidwinter cold brings hard times

ith the onset of winter, the hunters are less selective in their
uest for food. Although their store of dried meat will keep
em alive in times of dearth, they still go out in search of game.
rctic hares and foxes are trapped, and occasionally an Arctic
ouse. But as the nights become longer and the cold more
enetrating, more time is spent in the warmth of the tent, and
uring their waking hours the men try their hands at modelling
e animals they have met on numerous hunting trips, or

decorating bone bracelets. The more serious business of making weapons is also undertaken. Straight wooden spear-shafts are fashioned to replace broken ones, and sharp points of flint are set into the wood, secured with pitch made from the sap of the birch tree, and bound round with fine sinews. There will be weapons for everyone when the herds return in the spring.

Death a time for sorrow and mourning

The death of a member of the Gravettian group, whether through a hunting accident or old age, is an occasion for a solemn feast and a series of dances to mark the dead man's departure. The corpse is laid out dressed in his finest clothes and decorated with bracelets, necklaces and charms. When the dance of death has reached its solemn climax, the body is carried shoulder high to the oval grave and, as a final mark of respect, it is sprinkled with powder ground from a blood-red ochre to ensure continued life in the next world.

To a new camp

After a number of years at the same settlement, the Gravettians will seek new and perhaps better hunting grounds. They will move from their home settlement, and leave behind them the remains of their huts, the broken and discarded weapons and numerous broken animal bones. The ash of their burnt-out fires and even the bodies of their dead heroes will then be covered with the dust of 250 centuries.

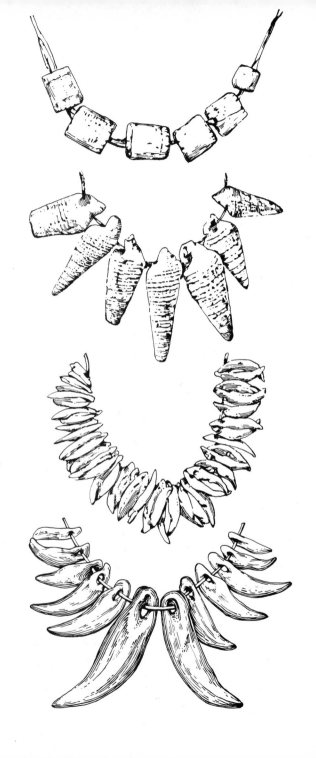

right: *Some of man's first personal ornaments, found in Czechoslovakia. These necklaces are made of pieces of elephant tusks, snail shells, fox and wolf teeth, and, at the bottom, bear teeth. As far as is known, Latest Man was the first man to wear 'jewellery' as elaborate as this.*

Ten thousand years pass: a Magdalenian cave

Let us now move forward in time to visit a Magdalenian hunting camp. You notice at once a number of differences from a Gravettian camp. In the first place, the Magdalenians occupy the forefront of a cave which commands a ford over an otherwise dangerous river. The rocky overhang of the cave entrance offers protection from the snow and rain, while in front a skin wind-break has been built. Such protection is vital, for the climate has worsened since Gravettian days. The choice of this cave has been a happy one. Every spring and autumn, migrating herds of reindeer cross the river at this point. Slowed down as they swim, they fall an easy prey to the waiting hunters. In summer the hunters disperse over the warm tundra landscape but they always return in time for the reindeer hunt.

A ceremony for new hunters

It is now early spring, and the reindeer are expected soon. In the meantime, three young men have attained an age when they must be initiated into the techniques and rites of hunting. The moon is barely up as the old chief, his face hidden behind an awesome bison-mask, enters the narrow passageway which leads to the inner sanctuary of the cave. He is preceded by two torch-bearers, while behind winds a procession of silent hunters, their bodies patterned in coloured symbols, and each with a mask less ornate than that of their chief, but just as strange. Finally come the three young men, dressed in garments suited to their impending status as full hunters. Now they have reached the inner cavern. The walls, which are faintly lit by dim lamps, reveal great animal paintings which seem almost to come alive and move in the flickering light. Here is a herd of deer, swimming across a stream, and there a great black bull, its head proudly erect. Notice also the symbolic signs painted on

the cave walls, heralding good fortune in the lifetime of hunting ahead.

The strange death of a clay bear

Listen: the drumming has begun, and the men begin dancing to the echoing rhythm. Slowly at first, but with ever increasing speed, the dance progresses until the sweat glistens on the swaying figures although the cave walls are freezing to the touch. At last, the chief signals for the dancing to halt, then, at a further sign, all present pick up spears and plunge them deep into the clay model of a bear, whose stone eyes glint mockingly into the gloom.

It seems as if the initiation has lasted but a few minutes, yet when the participants return to the cave front, the glimmer of the dawn shows in the eastern sky.

Spring brings the returning herds

The following week, scouts report that the first reindeer have been sighted. The camp is now very busy, as harpoons are

brought out for last-minute adjustments, and new spear-throwers are tested for unseen faults. The excitement reaches a climax when the first reindeer are finally seen approaching the far bank. At first, the wary animals hesitate, as if sensing the danger all around them, but when the leading stag forges ahead into the water, it is not long before the river is alive with swimming animals. Now is the time for a cool brain and a strong arm. The herd will soon be across and away, and as many reindeer as possible must be killed. When the herd is in midstream, the attack begins.

The riot of killing does not stop until the last animal is out of reach. When the time comes to count the toll, twenty-five animals lie stretched out on the river bank.

Antler, skin, bone: harpoons, tents, needles

No part of the dead reindeer is wasted. First the antler is hacked off: it will be used to make more harpoon-heads. Then the animals are skinned and the skins stacked in a heap ready for scraping and drying. The meat is then cut off the carcases. Some will be eaten the same evening, but the rest will be dried in the sun and stored, until men go out on hunting trips and need to carry several days' food with them. Bones and sinew remain. The skull will be smashed open to obtain the tasty brain, while

the bones will be kept to make needles and awls. Sinews are essential for stitching together skins to make clothing, and for binding spearheads to wooden shafts.

After many generations, the Ice Age ends

The Magdalenian hunters may well have felt that their way of life would continue for ever. For as long as they could remember, the reindeer herds had come north with spring, and returned again in autumn, supplying them with all the required. But, gradually, the weather began to improve. The glaciers slowly melted and retreated northwards. Trees began to cover the open countryside—first birch and pine, then oak, ash and elm. Some of the Magdalenians followed the ice and the reindeer, while others stayed behind, changing their way of life to the conditions offered by the new woodland and the animals it harboured. Yet the departure of the reindeer spelt the end of the Magdalenian people as we know them. New animals meant a new way of life. Warmth brought hunters out of the caverns into the open, and new hunting methods were developed, to track down the wily red deer, or to fish in the open lakes and along the seashores.

With this final retreat of the ice, we come to the end of what is known as the Old Stone Age.

3 THE ACHIEVEMENTS OF STONE AGE HUNTERS

Tools and weapons

In reading about what life must have been like during the period known as the Old Stone Age, you will have noticed that a number of important discoveries were made. Take, for example, the great increase in the variety of tools and weapons made by each of the successive types of man. It required considerably more skill on the part of Upright Man to make the multi-purpose handaxes than to make the simple chipped pebbles of his predecessors.

With Neanderthal Man, we find that points and scrapers were made by trimming carefully prepared flakes of stone, rather than directly from the large and clumsy parent nodule.

In developing the technique whereby long, parallel-sided blades of flint could be made, Latest Man was able to join small but exceedingly sharp fragments of stone to wooden hafts, thus making spears, arrows and knives. This continual, though very gradual, growth in the skills of Old Stone Age stone-workers ensured greater success in the hunt, and thus more food and essential raw materials, such as bone, leather and sinew.

Fire

You will also have seen how certain discoveries, which we now take for granted, changed our ancestors' way of life. Imagine, for example, what must have followed from Upright Man's discovery of how to make and control fire. Fire would at once have provided welcome warmth, as well as protection from wild animals. You can cook meat with fire, and harden the points of wooden spears by turning them in the dying embers. Yet Handy Man seems to have lived for a million and a half years without harnessing the many advantages of fire.

Colder lands

If Neanderthal Man had not invented clothing and had been without fire, then he would never have been able to survive in the cold parts of the world. Man the hunter has always been deeply influenced by the animals and plants which surround him. If the climate becomes colder, those plants and animals which provide him with his food will also change, leaving man two alternatives. Either he seeks the surroundings to which he is accustomed in another part of the world, or he remains where he is and changes his way of life to suit the new conditions around him. Equipped with a knowledge of fire, and dressed in warm skins, Neanderthal Man would have been able to stay in the cold regions of the world had he so wished. Indeed, this is exactly what appears to have happened to Neanderthal Man in Europe, for when the climate began to get colder, and animals to which he was accustomed moved away to the south, Neanderthal Man stayed on, adapting himself to the cold conditions.

The dead and the next life

It is also with Neanderthal Man that we have the first evidence of the reverence for the dead, and care for the infirm, which we now associate with human behaviour. The first evidence of these attitudes is most important, because it tells us when man first began to think about a life after death, and about the welfare of friends as well as of himself alone. With Neanderthal Man some people at least began to acquire an outlook on life which we now recognise as humane. Let us not, however, see Neanderthal Man as being invariably friendly to all: the grim remains of a cannibal feast at Krapina rule that out.

Ritual and paintings

Latest Man made clothes and cared for his fellows. But he is also remembered for his greatly improved skill at making tools, and for the development of a masterly form of art. It is perhaps hard for us today, surrounded as we are by all manner of drawings and paintings, to realise that the very discovery of painting was made by Latest Man over 25,000 years ago. In his paintings, we can catch a glimpse of his approach to life. We saw that magic dances were performed to bring good fortune in the hunt, so that unseen spirits might guide the hand of the spear-man, or direct home arrows into the running animal. Just like the Australian Aborigines today, Latest Man visualised a world beyond that which he could hear, see and touch. At the same time, he was attracted by the beauty of the world around him, for look at the masterly care with which the bison of Altamira were painted, and the delicate necklaces made to adorn the living, and accompany the dead to the grave. The

belief in a spirit world, and a delight in his surroundings mar out Latest Man from the hunters who preceded him on eart

It is hardly surprising, although still most exciting, to see tha people changed in appearance during the Old Stone Age. W have seen how it is possible to recognise the different types man. We would hardly recognise the first two as being human all, but for their ability to make simple tools of stone and woo But by gradual stages, they came to look increasingly like us features, if not in dress and customs.

The Old Stone Age draws to its close

The line marking the end of the Old Stone Age correspon to the end of the Ice Age, which was about ten thousand yea ago. By that time, Latest Man inhabited much of the worl adapting his way of life to the animals and plants around hir

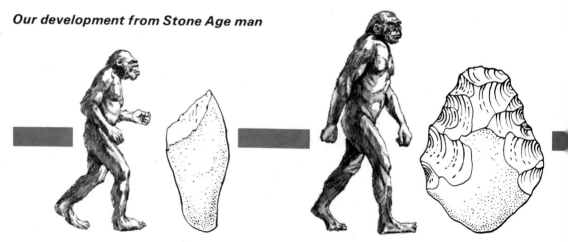

Our development from Stone Age man

By 2,500,000 years ago, Handy Man

By 1,500,000 years ago, Upright Man

some areas, however, such as the lower slopes of the Zagros Mountains in Iran, men were beginning to realise that by cultivating grain plants and herding animals, they could feed more people. By the end of the Old Stone Age, some men were on the brink of becoming farmers instead of hunters.

It seems surprising to read that Latest Man had discovered much of the world by the end of the Old Stone Age. Indeed, many people in Europe are accustomed to believe that it was Columbus who discovered America in 1492. But let us not forget that Columbus found America already inhabited, while Cortés found a civilised people, known as the Aztecs, living in Mexico when he arrived there in 1519. It is now well known that both the American Indians encountered by Columbus, and the Aztecs conquered by Cortés, were descended from hunters who crossed from Asia to America at least 20,000 years ago and perhaps much earlier, when the continents were joined by a narrow belt of land.

History books also record that a Dutchman, Captain Jantsz, discovered Australia in 1606. Again, the men of the Old Stone

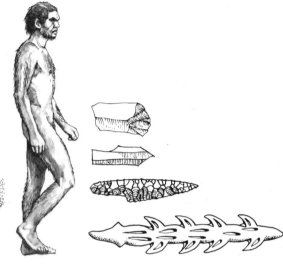

By 40,000 years ago, Latest Man

By 250,000 years ago, Thinking Man

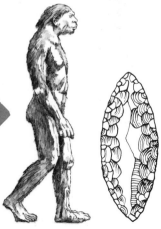

By 80,000 years ago, Neanderthal Man

Age were the first to land on that continent. Indeed some ancestors of the Aborigines had crossed over from New Guinea to Australia by about 40,000 years ago. Thus the Old Stone Age hunters came to occupy most of the world. Only the long ocean voyages, for example to the more remote Pacific Islands and New Zealand, as well as the discovery of the frozen wastes of Antarctica, remained to be accomplished when the Ice Age drew to a close.

In the time chart, you can see that we know approximately when each type of man emerged. Now think of the discoveries made by each type, and you will see that the most intelligent – Latest Man – has made easily the most discoveries and all in the comparatively short time of 40,000 years. Indeed, when the first groups of Latest Man lived, not even the bow and arrow were known, but now we can send a rocket to the moon. All the major inventions seem to have been made by Latest Man, from farming and the wheel to lasers and the hydrogen bomb.

However, we all know that no discovery is made without relying on earlier discoveries made by other people. How, for example, could Newcomen have invented his steam engine if someone else had not invented the process of making iron from iron-ore? How could Fleming have discovered penicillin without the aid of the microscope? In looking at the simple stone tools made countless centuries ago by the men of the Old Stone Age, therefore, we should see in them the first steps on a road which has led to our own scientific discoveries. Those distant ancestors made the initial discoveries – how to control fire, and make tools, clothes and shelter. Later men found out how to tame animals and to plant cereals. Without all these discoveries our own way of life would not have developed. Therefore, if the surviving traces of the men of the Old Stone Age and the tools they made seem simple and insignificant, try to imagine what our descendants a million years hence may think of what remains of our homes and cities, and how strange our way of life may seem to have been.

An Australian Aborigine, Sam of Millingimbi, paints on a panel o bark the life-cycle of two mythical sisters important to the artist's tribe.

back cover: *The painting shows in the bottom panel the sisters surrounded by four mats on which females are laid after birth. In the second, accompanied by their brother, they watch a sunset and a sunrise; beside them are sacred emblems decorated with feathers, and four sacred trees. The third panel shows the sisters giving birth to the people of their tribe: males yellow, females black. Lastly, the sisters lie in their graves, while beside them the artist sings tribal songs, accompanying himself on a goanna rangga, an instrument with feathered strings.*